A Joyous Celebration for Two

Piano and Organ Duets for Almost Any Season
Vol. 2 - God & Country

Arrangements by Ellen Foncannon

John Rich Music Press

EXCLUSIVELY DISTRIBUTED BY
HAL•LEONARD®

*A JOYOUS CELEBRATION FOR TWO is dedicated to
my dear friend and duet partner, Judy Marshall.
Her strong faith, talented hands, gentle spirit and
precious friendship have shaped both me and this music.
"May the favor of the Lord our God rest upon us;
establish the work of our hands..." Ps. 90:17*

A Joyous Celebration for Two

Arrangements by Ellen Foncannon

Table of Contents

God of Our Fathers
with
America the Beautiful

George Warren/Samuel Ward
Arranged by Ellen Foncannon

Sw. Trumpets 8', 4'
Gt. Full Foundations, no Reeds
Ped. Diap. 8', Fl 16', 8', 4'

JR7020

We Gather Together

with
Largo

G. F. Handel
NETHERLANDS FOLK HYMN
Arranged by Ellen Foncannon

Sw. Clarinet, Flute 8'
Gt. Soft celeste strings
Ped. Flute 16', 8'

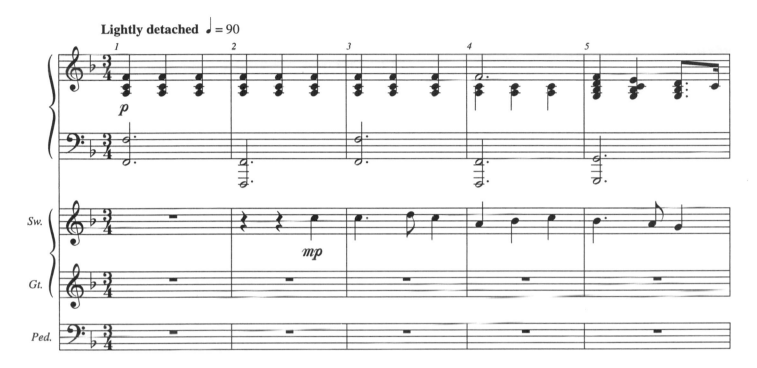

JR7020

Praise to the Lord

LOBE DEN HERREN
Arranged by Ellen Foncannon

Sw. Diapason, Flute 8', Trumpet 8'
Gt. Diapason 8', 4', Flute 8', 4'
Ped. Principal 8', Flute 16', 8'

Joyfully, with crisp articulation

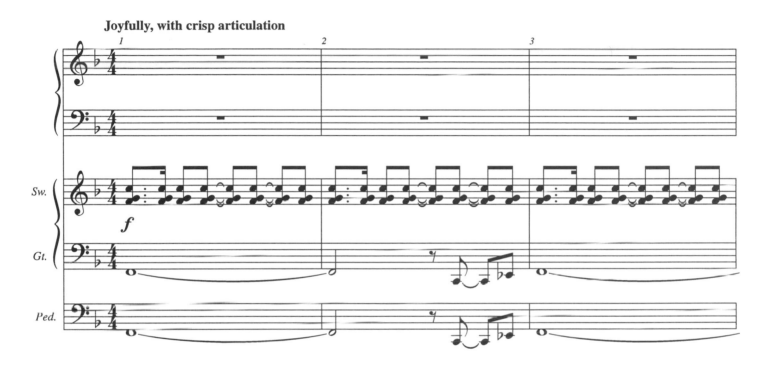

JR7020

14

Lead On, O King Eternal

with
Onward, Christian Soldiers

Henry Smart
Arranged by Ellen Foncannon

Sw. Trumpets 8', 4'
Gt. Full Foundations
Ped. 16', 8'

JR7020

Exclusively Distributed By

HAL•LEONARD®
CORPORATION

7777 W. Bluemound Rd. P.O. Box 13819 Milwaukee, WI 53213

0 73999 39705 5